How to Make Money in 2024 and 2025 from Affiliate Links

Introduction

Affiliate marketing has become one of the most effective and accessible ways to generate income online, and its popularity shows no sign of slowing down as we move into 2024 and 2025.

The essence of affiliate marketing lies in promoting products or services from other companies and earning a commission for every sale, click, or lead generated through your referral.

This model appeals to a wide range of people, from bloggers and influencers to entrepreneurs and marketers, because of its flexibility, scalability, and relatively low barrier to entry.

In the past decade, affiliate marketing has evolved significantly. It has gone from a niche strategy to a mainstream income stream that generates billions of dollars in revenue each year.

As digital commerce expands and consumer behavior continues to shift online, the opportunities in affiliate marketing are poised to grow even further.

The rise of social media, influencer culture, and content marketing has opened up new avenues for affiliates to reach audiences and drive conversions.

As we look toward 2024 and 2025, several trends are shaping the future of affiliate marketing. These include the increasing importance of micro-influencers, the growth of mobile and social commerce, and the integration of AI and machine learning in marketing strategies.

Additionally, the industry is adapting to new regulations and a growing focus on data privacy, which are important considerations for anyone looking to succeed in affiliate marketing.

In this comprehensive guide, we will delve into the details of how you can make money through affiliate marketing in 2024 and 2025.

From understanding the basics to selecting a profitable niche, building a platform, generating traffic, and scaling your efforts, this guide will provide you with the knowledge and tools you need to thrive in the ever-evolving world of affiliate marketing.

Chapter 1: Understanding Affiliate Marketing Basics

What is Affiliate Marketing?

Affiliate marketing is a performance-based marketing strategy where individuals (affiliates) promote products or services offered by another company (merchant) and earn a commission for each action taken by the consumers they refer.

This action could be a sale, a click, or a lead, depending on the terms of the affiliate program.

The key players in the affiliate marketing ecosystem include:

1. Affiliates:

These are the marketers or publishers who promote the merchant's products.

Affiliates can be bloggers, influencers, content creators, or website owners.

2. Merchants:

These are the companies or individuals who own the products or services being promoted.

They offer affiliate programs that detail the terms of the partnership, including the commission structure and payment terms.

3. Affiliate Networks:

 These platforms act as intermediaries between affiliates and merchants.

 They provide a centralized place for affiliates to find products to promote, track performance, and manage payments.

 Examples include ShareASale, CJ Affiliate, and Rakuten Marketing.

4. Consumers:

These are the end-users who interact with the affiliate's content, click on the affiliate links, and make purchases or take other actions.

How Affiliate Marketing Works

The process of affiliate marketing typically follows these steps:

1. Affiliate Joins an Affiliate Program:

The affiliate selects a program that aligns with their niche or audience.

This could be directly with a merchant or through an affiliate network.

2. Affiliate Promotes the Products:

 The affiliate creates content (blogs, videos, social media posts, etc.) that includes affiliate links to the merchant's products.

3. Consumers Click on Affiliate Links:

 When the affiliate's audience engages with the content and clicks on the links, they are redirected to the merchant's website.

4. Consumers Take Action:

If the consumer makes a purchase, signs up for a service, or completes another desired action, the affiliate earns a commission.

5. Merchant Confirms the Sale:

The merchant tracks the affiliate's performance and confirms the sale or action, ensuring that it qualifies for a commission.

6. Affiliate Gets Paid:

Based on the terms of the affiliate program, the affiliate is paid for their efforts, usually through a network or directly from the merchant.

Different Types of Affiliate Marketing

- Pay-per-Sale:

 The affiliate earns a commission for each sale generated through their link.

 This is the most common type of affiliate marketing, where affiliates are paid a percentage of the sale value. It's widely used because it aligns the affiliate's goals with the merchant's, ensuring that both parties benefit from successful conversions.

- Pay-per-Click (PPC):

In this model, affiliates are paid based on the number of clicks their affiliate links receive, regardless of whether those clicks result in a sale.

This method can be profitable for affiliates with high-traffic platforms but often requires a more strategic approach to ensure the clicks are valuable to the merchant.

- Pay-per-Lead (PPL):

Affiliates earn a commission for generating leads for the merchant, such as filling out a form, signing up for a trial, or subscribing to a newsletter.

This model is common in industries where customer acquisition is a lengthy process, such as financial services, education, or software.

- Pay-per-Install (PPI):

This model is specific to software and app promotions, where affiliates are paid each time a user installs the software or app through their link.

It's a popular model for promoting mobile apps and downloadable software.

Why Choose Affiliate Marketing?

Affiliate marketing offers several unique advantages that make it an attractive income stream for many individuals and businesses, particularly in 2024 and 2025.

Here are some of the key reasons why you might choose to enter this field:

- Low Startup Costs:

One of the biggest appeals of affiliate marketing is that it requires minimal upfront investment.

You don't need to create your own products, hold inventory, or handle shipping.

Your main costs might include building and hosting a website, creating content, and potentially investing in advertising.

- Flexibility:

 Affiliate marketing allows you to work from anywhere with an internet connection.

 Whether you want to work part-time as a side hustle or full-time, it's entirely up to you.

 This flexibility makes it an appealing option for digital nomads, stay-at-home parents, and anyone looking for work-life balance.

- Scalability:

As your affiliate marketing business grows, it becomes more scalable.

You can promote more products, enter new niches, and even build a team to help you expand.

Your income potential can grow exponentially without a corresponding increase in time or effort.

- Passive Income Potential:

While it takes time and effort to build up your affiliate marketing channels, once established, they can generate passive income.

Evergreen content, for example, can continue to drive traffic and sales long after it's published, providing a steady stream of income.

- Global Reach:

The internet allows you to reach audiences all over the world.

Unlike a traditional business limited by location, affiliate marketing enables you to tap into global markets.

This can be especially lucrative if you promote digital products or services that have universal appeal.

Trends Shaping Affiliate Marketing in 2024-2025

As we move further into 2024 and look toward 2025, several trends are emerging that will shape the affiliate marketing landscape.

Staying ahead of these trends will be crucial for anyone looking to succeed in this competitive field.

1. Rise of Micro-Influencers

Micro-influencers, typically defined as social media users with 1,000 to 100,000 followers, are gaining prominence in the affiliate marketing world.

These influencers often have highly engaged audiences and niche-specific followings, making them valuable partners for brands looking to reach targeted consumers. In 2024 and 2025, leveraging micro-influencers can be a powerful strategy for affiliates, especially in niche markets.

2. Increased Mobile Commerce and Social Commerce

Mobile commerce (m-commerce) is expected to account for an even larger share of e-commerce sales in 2024 and 2025.

With the majority of consumers using smartphones to shop online, affiliates must optimize their content and links for mobile users.

Additionally, social commerce—buying products directly through social media platforms—is becoming increasingly popular.

Platforms like Instagram, TikTok, and Pinterest are integrating shopping features, providing new opportunities for affiliates to monetize their social media presence.

3. Integration of AI and Machine Learning

Artificial Intelligence (AI) and machine learning are transforming how affiliates approach marketing. These technologies can help affiliates optimize their campaigns by analyzing vast amounts of data to identify trends, predict consumer behavior, and personalize content. AI-driven tools can also automate repetitive tasks, such as email marketing or ad placements, allowing affiliates to focus on strategy and creativity.

4. Growing Focus on Data Privacy and Ethical Marketing

Data privacy is a major concern for consumers, and regulations like GDPR in Europe and CCPA in California have set new standards for how personal data is collected and used. Affiliates need to be transparent about data usage and ensure they comply with these regulations. Additionally, ethical marketing practices—such as disclosing affiliate relationships and promoting products honestly—are increasingly important in building trust with audiences.

Chapter 2: Choosing Your Niche

Why Niche Selection is Crucial

Selecting the right niche is one of the most important decisions you'll make as an affiliate marketer.

Your niche will determine the type of content you create, the products you promote, and the audience you attract.

Here's why choosing a niche is so crucial:

- Understanding Audience-Specific Needs:

A well-defined niche allows you to focus on a specific audience with particular needs, interests, and pain points.

By understanding your audience deeply, you can create content and promotions that resonate with them, leading to higher engagement and conversion rates.

- Competitive Analysis and Market Saturation:

 Some niches are more competitive than others. While entering a highly competitive niche can be challenging, it can also be rewarding if you can differentiate yourself.

 Conversely, less competitive niches may offer easier entry but might have lower earning potential. Conducting a thorough competitive analysis will help you strike the right balance.

- Balancing Passion with Profitability:

It's important to choose a niche that you're passionate about because you'll be creating a lot of content around it.

However, passion alone isn't enough—you also need to ensure that the niche is profitable.

Ideally, your niche should be something you enjoy and have the potential to generate income.

Top Profitable Niches in 2024 and 2025

While countless niches can be profitable, some stand out as particularly lucrative in 2024 and 2025 due to current trends and consumer demand.

Here are some top niches to consider:

1. Health and Wellness

- Sub-niches:
Fitness, nutrition, mental health, supplements, yoga, and meditation.

- Why it's profitable:
The health and wellness industry is booming as more people prioritize their physical and mental well-being. The pandemic has also heightened awareness of health issues, leading to increased demand for products and services that promote a healthy lifestyle.

2. Technology

- Sub-niches:
Gadgets, software, SaaS products, cybersecurity, smart home devices.

- Why it's profitable:
Technology is constantly evolving, creating endless opportunities for affiliates. Consumers are always looking for the latest gadgets and tools to enhance their lives, and businesses are investing heavily in technology solutions, making this a highly profitable niche.

3. Finance and Investing

- Sub-niches:
Personal finance, cryptocurrency, stock trading, credit repair, insurance.

- Why it's profitable:
As more people seek financial independence and security, the demand for financial products and advice is growing.

The rise of cryptocurrency and other alternative investments has also opened up new opportunities for affiliates in this space.

4. Green Living and Sustainability

- Sub-niches:
Eco-friendly products, renewable energy, sustainable fashion, organic food.

- Why it's profitable:
Consumers are becoming more environmentally conscious, leading to increased demand for sustainable products and services. Brands that prioritize sustainability are seeing strong growth, and affiliates can capitalize on this trend by promoting green living solutions.

5. Education and Online Learning

- Sub-niches:
 Online courses, eBooks, skill development, language learning, professional certifications.

- Why it's profitable:
 The shift toward online education is accelerating, with more people turning to digital platforms to acquire new skills. This niche offers a wide range of products to promote, from online courses to educational software, making it a highly profitable area for affiliates.

How to Validate Your Niche

Once you've identified a potential niche, it's important to validate it to ensure it has the potential to generate income.

Here are some steps to validate your niche:

1. Analyze Search Volume and Trends:

 Use tools like Google Trends, SEMrush, or Ahrefs to analyze the search volume for keywords related to your niche.

 Look for consistent or growing interest in your chosen niche over time.

 High search volume indicates strong demand, while a growing trend suggests future potential.

2. Competitor Research:

Identify other affiliates and content creators in your niche and analyze their strategies.

Look at the type of content they produce, the products they promote, and how they engage with their audience.

Competitor research will give you insights into what's working and where there might be gaps in the market.

3. Testing the Waters:

Before fully committing to a niche, you can test its viability by creating some initial content or engaging with potential audiences on social media.

This can help you gauge interest and refine your approach before investing more time and resources.

Chapter 3: Building a Platform for Affiliate Marketing

Setting Up Your Website or Blog

Your website or blog will be the central hub of your affiliate marketing efforts.

It's where you'll publish content, promote affiliate products, and engage with your audience.

Here's how to set up a website or blog that's optimized for affiliate marketing:

1. Choosing the Right Domain and Hosting

- Your domain name should be relevant to your niche, easy to remember, and professional.

 Avoid using numbers or hyphens, as they can make your domain harder to remember.

Choosing a reliable hosting provider is crucial for ensuring your website runs smoothly.

Look for hosting services that offer good uptime, fast load speeds, and excellent customer support.

Popular options include Bluehost, SiteGround, and WP Engine, especially if you're using WordPress as your content management system (CMS).

2. Website Design Best Practices for Affiliate Marketing

- User Experience (UX):

 Your website should be easy to navigate, with a clean layout that allows visitors to find information quickly.

 Focus on creating a smooth user experience with a clear hierarchy of content, intuitive menus, and fast-loading pages.

- Mobile Optimization:

 With the majority of web traffic coming from mobile devices, it's essential that your website is mobile-friendly.

 Use responsive design techniques to ensure that your site looks great and functions well on all devices.

- Call to Action (CTA) Placement:

Strategic placement of CTAs is key to maximizing conversions.

Whether it's a button to click through to a product page or a subscription box for your email list, CTAs should be prominent and compelling, encouraging visitors to take action.

3. Essential Plugins and Tools

- SEO Plugins:

 Tools like Yoast SEO or Rank Math help you optimize your content for search engines, improving your chances of ranking higher in search results.

- Analytics Tools:

 Google Analytics is essential for tracking your site's performance, visitor behavior, and conversions. This data will help you refine your strategies over time.

- Affiliate Link Management:

Plugins like ThirstyAffiliates or Pretty Links allow you to manage and cloak your affiliate links, making them more attractive and easier to track.

Creating Engaging Content

Content is the lifeblood of affiliate marketing.

High-quality, relevant content drives traffic, builds trust with your audience, and encourages conversions.

Here's how to create content that resonates:

1. Importance of High-Quality, Value-Driven Content

- Your content should provide real value to your audience.

 This could be in the form of solving a problem, offering advice, or sharing expertise.

 Value-driven content not only engages readers but also builds trust, which is crucial for successful affiliate marketing.

2. Content Types That Work Well with Affiliate Links

- Product Reviews:
 Detailed reviews of products can be very effective, especially if they include personal experiences, pros and cons, and comparisons with similar products.

- Tutorials and How-Tos:
 These types of content guide readers through a process and can naturally incorporate affiliate links as recommended tools or products.

- Comparison Posts:

 Side-by-side comparisons of similar products help readers make informed decisions and can include affiliate links to each option.

- Listicles:

 Lists like "Top 10 Gadgets for 2024" are popular and shareable, providing multiple opportunities to include affiliate links.

3. Content Calendar Planning and Consistency

- Plan your content in advance to ensure a steady flow of new posts. A content calendar helps you stay organized and ensures you cover a variety of topics that will interest your audience.

- Consistency is key to building an engaged audience. Whether you post weekly or bi-weekly, stick to a schedule that you can maintain over the long term.

Leveraging Social Media

 Social media platforms offer a powerful way to reach potential customers and drive traffic to your affiliate links.

 Here's how to effectively use social media for affiliate marketing:

1. Best Platforms for Affiliate Marketing in 2024 and 2025

- Instagram:
With features like Stories, Reels, and Shopping, Instagram is a great platform for promoting lifestyle products, fashion, beauty, and more.

- YouTube:
Video content is incredibly engaging, and YouTube's vast audience makes it a prime platform for tutorials, reviews, and unboxings that incorporate affiliate links.

- TikTok:
 Growing rapidly, TikTok is ideal for short, catchy videos that can go viral and drive significant traffic.

- Pinterest:
 Especially effective for niches like DIY, home decor, fashion, and recipes, Pinterest allows you to create visually appealing pins that link back to your content.

2. Strategies for Building a Following

- Consistency:

 Regular posting is key to growing your social media presence.

 Use scheduling tools like Buffer or Hootsuite to maintain a consistent posting schedule.

- Engagement:

Actively engage with your audience by responding to comments, participating in conversations, and asking questions to foster a sense of community.

- Collaborations:

Partnering with other influencers or brands in your niche can help you reach new audiences and build credibility.

3. Using Social Media Analytics to Refine Your Approach

- Each social media platform offers analytics tools that provide insights into your content's performance, audience demographics, and engagement rates.

 Use this data to adjust your strategy, focusing on what resonates most with your audience.

Chapter 4: Generating Traffic

SEO for Affiliate Marketing

Search engine optimization (SEO) is critical for driving organic traffic to your affiliate website.

Here's how to optimize your content to rank higher in search engine results:

1. On-Page SEO Techniques

- Keyword Research:
 Identify high-traffic keywords relevant to your niche using tools like Ahrefs, SEMrush, or Ubersuggest.

 Focus on long-tail keywords that are less competitive but highly relevant.

- Meta Tags:

 Optimize your title tags, meta descriptions, and header tags with target keywords.

 These elements help search engines understand your content and improve click-through rates.

- Internal Linking:

 Use internal links to connect related content on your site.

 This helps search engines crawl your site more effectively and encourages visitors to explore more of your content.

2. Off-Page SEO Techniques

- Backlink Building:

Acquiring high-quality backlinks from reputable sites signals to search engines that your content is valuable, improving your rankings.

Guest blogging, influencer outreach, and creating shareable content are effective backlink strategies.

- Social Signals:

 While not a direct ranking factor, social media activity can drive traffic to your site, leading to increased visibility and potential backlinks.

3. Keyword Research for Affiliate Content

- Focus on finding keywords with high search intent. For example, keywords like "best [product] for [purpose]" or "[product] reviews" indicate that users are close to making a purchase decision.

- Use tools like Google Keyword Planner to identify keywords with a good balance of search volume and competition.

4. Link-Building Strategies

- Guest Blogging:
 Write high-quality articles for other websites in your niche, including links back to your content.
- Influencer Outreach:
 Collaborate with influencers who can link to your site or share your content with their audience.
- Content Marketing:
 Create valuable, shareable content like infographics, eBooks, or research reports that others in your industry will want to link to.

Paid Advertising Options

While SEO is a powerful tool for long-term traffic, paid advertising can provide immediate results.

Here's how to leverage paid advertising for affiliate marketing:

1. Google Ads

- Search Ads:
Bid on keywords relevant to your niche to display ads in Google search results. Target high-intent keywords to attract users who are ready to buy.

- Display Ads:
Use Google's Display Network to place banner ads on relevant websites. This can help increase brand awareness and drive targeted traffic to your affiliate content.

2. Facebook and Instagram Ads

- Targeting:
Use Facebook's robust targeting options to reach specific demographics, interests, and behaviors. This ensures your ads are seen by people most likely to convert.

- Retargeting:
Implement retargeting campaigns to reach users who have visited your site but haven't converted. This can be an effective way to recapture potential customers.

3. Affiliate-Friendly PPC Strategies

- Focus on promoting high-converting offers with clear benefits. Your ad copy should be compelling and highlight the value of the product or service.

- Track your ad performance closely, using tools like Google Analytics and Facebook Ads Manager to monitor conversions and ROI. Adjust your campaigns based on performance data to maximize effectiveness.

Email Marketing

Email marketing remains one of the most effective ways to drive traffic and conversions in affiliate marketing.

Here's how to build and optimize your email campaigns:

1. Building and Growing Your Email List

- Lead Magnets:
 Offer valuable content like eBooks, checklists, or exclusive discounts in exchange for email sign-ups. Make sure your lead magnets are highly relevant to your niche.

- Opt-In Forms:
 Place opt-in forms strategically on your website, such as in the header, sidebar, or at the end of blog posts. Use compelling copy to encourage sign-ups.

2. Crafting Effective Affiliate Email Campaigns

- Personalization:
 Use your email marketing platform's personalization features to address subscribers by name and tailor content based on their preferences or behavior.

- Segmentation:
 Segment your list based on factors like purchase history, engagement level, or interests. This allows you to send more targeted and relevant content, increasing the likelihood of conversions.

- Content Mix:

 Balance promotional content with value-driven content to keep your audience engaged.

 For example, send a mix of product recommendations, helpful tips, and exclusive deals.

3. Segmenting Your List for Personalized Offers

- Use behavioral data to create segments within your email list. For example, you could create segments for users who have clicked on certain types of products, opened specific emails, or visited particular pages on your site.

- Tailor your offers to each segment. For instance, if a segment is highly interested in fitness, promote health and wellness products to them, rather than unrelated offers.

Chapter 5: Optimizing for Conversions

Understanding the Buyer's Journey

The buyer's journey is the process consumers go through from the moment they become aware of a product or service to the point of making a purchase.

Understanding this journey is crucial for optimizing your affiliate marketing strategy, as it allows you to create content that addresses the specific needs of your audience at each stage.

1. Awareness Stage

- In the awareness stage, potential customers realize they have a problem or need but aren't yet sure what solution they require. Your content should focus on educating the audience and making them aware of potential solutions.

- Content Types:
 Blog posts, educational videos, and social media content that discusses common problems or needs in your niche.

2. Consideration Stage

- In this stage, the audience has identified their problem and is actively looking for solutions. They are comparing different products or services to find the best fit.

- Content Types:
 Product comparisons, in-depth reviews, how-to guides, and case studies that highlight the benefits and features of the products you're promoting.

3. Decision Stage

- At the decision stage, the audience is ready to make a purchase. Your content should focus on making the final push, highlighting why the product you're promoting is the best choice.

- Content Types:
 Detailed product reviews, testimonials, exclusive discount offers, and CTA-focused landing pages.

4. Using A/B Testing for Optimization

- A/B testing involves creating two versions of a piece of content (such as a landing page or email) to see which one performs better. You can test different headlines, CTAs, images, and content layouts to determine what resonates most with your audience.
  - Regularly conduct A/B testing to refine your content and improve conversion rates. Even small changes can lead to significant increases in conversions over time.

Effective Use of Affiliate Links

Maximizing the effectiveness of your affiliate links is essential for generating income.

Here's how to use them strategically:

1. Placement Strategies for Higher Click-Through Rates (CTR)

- In-Content Links:
 Placing links within the body of your content tends to generate higher CTRs compared to banners or sidebar ads.

 Embed affiliate links naturally within your articles, especially in product reviews or tutorials.

- Multiple Touchpoints:

 Don't rely on a single link to drive conversions.

 Include affiliate links at multiple points throughout your content, such as in introductions, within key sections, and in conclusion or CTA sections.

- Contextual Relevance:

 Ensure your affiliate links are relevant to the surrounding content.

 If your audience finds the links useful and related to what they're reading, they're more likely to click through.

2. Link Cloaking and Tracking Tools

- Link Cloaking:

Tools like Pretty Links or ThirstyAffiliates allow you to "cloak" your affiliate links, making them shorter, more attractive, and easier to remember.

For example, instead of a long URL, you can use a branded link like yoursite.com/recommendation.

- Tracking Tools:

  Use tracking tools to monitor the performance of your affiliate links.

  Platforms like Google Analytics, ClickMeter, or the built-in analytics of your affiliate network can show you which links are generating the most clicks and conversions.

  Use this data to optimize your link placement and promotional strategies.

3. Complying with FTC Guidelines and Disclosure Rules

- Transparency is critical in affiliate marketing. The Federal Trade Commission (FTC) requires affiliates to disclose their relationships with merchants.

 This means you must clearly inform your audience that you may earn a commission from the links on your site.

- Place disclosures prominently on your website, such as at the beginning of blog posts, in the footer of your website, or as a popup.

 Ensure that your disclosure is clear and easy to understand, using straightforward language like "This post contains affiliate links. If you make a purchase through these links, I may earn a commission at no extra cost to you."

Leveraging Analytics and Data

To optimize your affiliate marketing efforts, it's essential to track and analyze your performance continuously.

Here's how to use analytics effectively:

1. Tools for Tracking Affiliate Performance

- Use Google Analytics to track key metrics such as page views, bounce rate, and conversion rate. Set up goals and funnels to monitor how visitors move through your site and where they drop off.
- Affiliate networks often provide their own analytics dashboards, where you can see detailed reports on clicks, conversions, and earnings. Use these insights to identify which products, campaigns, or content types are most effective.

2. Understanding Key Metrics

- Click-Through Rate (CTR):
 The percentage of visitors who click on your affiliate links. A higher CTR indicates that your content and link placement are compelling.
- Conversion Rate:
 The percentage of visitors who take a desired action, such as making a purchase, after clicking on your affiliate link. A higher conversion rate suggests that your audience finds value in the products you promote.

- Earnings Per Click (EPC): The average amount of money earned for each click on your affiliate links.

 This metric helps you evaluate the profitability of your campaigns and compare the performance of different products or programs.

3. Making Data-Driven Decisions to Improve ROI

- Regularly review your analytics to identify trends and areas for improvement.

 For example, if a particular piece of content has a high CTR but low conversion rate, consider whether the product being promoted aligns with your audience's needs.

- Use data to refine your content strategy, focusing more on the types of content, products, and promotional methods that generate the highest ROI.

Don't be afraid to experiment with new approaches, but always base your decisions on data to ensure you're optimizing your efforts effectively.

Chapter 6: Scaling Your Affiliate Marketing Business

Expanding Your Content Strategy

As your affiliate marketing business grows, expanding your content strategy is crucial for reaching new audiences and increasing revenue.

Here's how to scale your content efforts:

1. Diversifying Content Types

- Videos:

 Video content is highly engaging and can reach audiences who prefer visual or auditory learning.

 Create video reviews, unboxings, tutorials, and webinars that incorporate affiliate links.

 Platforms like YouTube and Vimeo are great for video marketing.

- Podcasts:

 If you're comfortable speaking and have valuable insights to share, consider starting a podcast.

 You can mention and recommend products during your episodes, directing listeners to your show notes for affiliate links.

- Infographics:

 Infographics are visually appealing and highly shareable, making them a great way to present complex information in an easy-to-digest format.

 Include affiliate links in your infographic or within the accompanying blog post.

2. Collaborations and Guest Posting

- Collaborations:

 Partner with other bloggers, influencers, or industry experts to create joint content.

 This could include co-hosted webinars, joint eBooks, or collaborative blog posts.

 Collaborations allow you to tap into each other's audiences and share affiliate commissions.

- Guest Posting:

 Writing guest posts for popular blogs in your niche is an excellent way to reach a new audience.

 Include your affiliate links in these posts where relevant, or link back to your website where your links are embedded in your content.

3. Creating Evergreen Content

- Evergreen content remains relevant and valuable over time, consistently driving traffic and conversions. Examples include how-to guides, comprehensive reviews, and in-depth tutorials that address timeless topics in your niche.
- Regularly update your evergreen content to ensure it remains accurate and includes up-to-date affiliate links. This ongoing maintenance will help your content continue to perform well in search engines and attract new visitors.

Outsourcing and Automation

As your affiliate marketing business scales, outsourcing and automation become essential for managing increased workload efficiently:

1. When and What to Outsource

- Content Creation:
If writing, video production, or graphic design isn't your forte, consider hiring freelancers or agencies to handle these tasks. This allows you to maintain a consistent content output while focusing on strategy and growth.

- Social Media Management: Managing multiple social media accounts can be time-consuming. Outsource this task to a social media manager who can handle posting, engagement, and analytics, freeing up your time for other activities.

- Administrative Tasks: Outsource routine tasks like email management, data entry, and bookkeeping to virtual assistants. This allows you to focus on high-impact activities that drive growth.

2. Tools for Automation

- Email Marketing:
Use email marketing platforms like Mailchimp, ConvertKit, or ActiveCampaign to automate your email campaigns.

Set up autoresponders, drip campaigns, and segmentation rules to ensure your subscribers receive timely and relevant content.

- Social Media Scheduling:
 Tools like Buffer, Hootsuite, or Later allow you to schedule social media posts in advance, ensuring consistent activity across all platforms.

- Content Automation:
 Tools like Zapier can automate repetitive tasks, such as sharing new blog posts to social media or updating a spreadsheet with new email subscribers. Automation saves time and reduces the risk of human error.

3. Managing Your Team and Workflow

- Use project management tools like Trello, Asana, or Monday.com to keep track of tasks, deadlines, and team responsibilities.

 Clear communication and organization are key to ensuring that your team works efficiently and meets deadlines.

- Regularly review your team's performance and provide feedback to ensure continuous improvement.

 Establish clear goals and KPIs (Key Performance Indicators) to measure success and adjust strategies as needed.

Diversifying Income Streams

Relying solely on one source of income can be risky.

Diversifying your income streams can provide financial stability and increase your earnings:

1. Adding Multiple Affiliate Programs

- Consider joining multiple affiliate programs to diversify your product offerings and income sources. This also allows you to compare the performance of different programs and choose the ones that offer the best commissions, support, and product alignment with your audience. Make sure that the programs you join complement each other and provide value to your readers rather than overwhelming them with too many options.

2. Exploring CPA Networks and High-Ticket Offers

- CPA (Cost Per Action) Networks:
CPA networks pay you for generating specific actions, such as sign-ups, downloads, or lead generation.

These actions often involve lower barriers to entry for consumers, which can result in higher conversion rates compared to traditional affiliate programs. Examples of CPA networks include MaxBounty and PeerFly.

- High-Ticket Offers:

  Promote high-ticket products or services that offer significantly higher commissions per sale.

  These could include premium software, online courses, coaching programs, or luxury items.

  While high-ticket items may have lower conversion rates, the higher payouts can substantially boost your income.

3. Building and Selling Your Own Products/Services Alongside Affiliate Marketing

- Digital Products:

 Create and sell digital products like eBooks, online courses, or software that align with your niche.

 These products can provide a recurring revenue stream and can be cross-promoted with your affiliate products.

- Consulting Services:

 If you have expertise in your niche, consider offering consulting or coaching services.

 This not only diversifies your income but also positions you as an authority in your field, which can boost your affiliate marketing efforts.

- Membership Sites:

 Build a membership site where users pay a recurring fee to access exclusive content, tools, or community features.

 This model allows you to create a loyal customer base while also promoting affiliate products within your membership offerings.

Chapter 7: Challenges and Pitfalls in Affiliate Marketing

Common Mistakes to Avoid

Even seasoned affiliate marketers can fall into common traps that hinder their success.

Here are some pitfalls to watch out for and how to avoid them:

1. Spamming Links and Neglecting Content Quality

- One of the biggest mistakes in affiliate marketing is overloading content with affiliate links without providing real value. Readers can quickly sense when content is purely promotional, leading to a loss of trust and engagement.

-Solution:

Focus on creating high-quality, informative content that genuinely helps your audience. Use affiliate links sparingly and only when they add value to the reader's experience.

2. Ignoring the Audience's Needs and Preferences

- If you're not attuned to your audience's needs, your promotions may fall flat. It's essential to understand what your audience is looking for and tailor your content and product recommendations accordingly.

- Solution:
 Engage with your audience regularly through comments, social media, and surveys. Pay attention to their feedback and adjust your strategies to better meet their expectations.

3. Over-Reliance on One Platform or Affiliate Program

- Relying too heavily on a single traffic source (e.g., Google search or Facebook) or affiliate program can be risky. Changes in algorithms, policies, or commission structures can dramatically impact your income.
- Solution:

 Diversify your traffic sources by investing in SEO, social media, email marketing, and paid advertising. Similarly, diversify your affiliate programs to reduce dependence on any single source of income.

Dealing with Competition

The affiliate marketing landscape is highly competitive, and standing out can be challenging.

Here's how to differentiate yourself and thrive even in saturated markets:

1. Finding Unique Angles in a Saturated Market

- To stand out in a crowded niche, look for unique angles or perspectives that others haven't covered. This could involve focusing on a sub-niche, addressing a specific problem, or providing a fresh take on common topics.
- Solution:

 Conduct thorough research to identify gaps in the content provided by competitors. Create content that offers a different perspective, better solutions, or more comprehensive information.

2. Building a Loyal Audience

- A loyal audience is your best asset in a competitive market. When your audience trusts and values your recommendations, they're more likely to follow your affiliate links and make purchases.

- Solution:
 Build relationships with your audience through consistent, valuable content, and active engagement. Respond to comments, provide personalized advice, and create a community around your brand.

3. Differentiating Through Branding and Personality

- Your personal brand and voice can be powerful differentiators. Even if you're covering similar topics as your competitors, your unique style, personality, and branding can attract a distinct audience.
- Solution:

 Develop a strong personal brand that reflects your values, expertise, and unique personality. Use consistent branding across your website, social media, and content to create a memorable identity.

Navigating Legal and Ethical Considerations

Operating within the legal and ethical boundaries of affiliate marketing is crucial for long-term success.

Here's how to stay compliant and build trust with your audience:

1. Understanding Affiliate Agreements

- Before promoting any product, carefully review the affiliate agreement. Understand the terms of payment, the commission structure, the allowed promotional methods, and any restrictions or requirements.
- Solution:

Keep detailed records of your affiliate agreements and periodically review them to ensure compliance. If you have any doubts or questions, contact the affiliate program's support team for clarification.

2. GDPR, CCPA, and Other Privacy Regulations

- Privacy regulations like GDPR (General Data Protection Regulation) in Europe and CCPA (California Consumer Privacy Act) in California have strict rules regarding the collection and use of personal data.

 Failure to comply can result in heavy fines and damage to your reputation.

- Solution:

 Ensure that your website has a clear privacy policy that complies with relevant regulations.

 Obtain explicit consent before collecting any personal data, and provide users with the option to opt-out of data collection.

 Consider using a cookie consent tool to manage user permissions.

3. Ethical Marketing Practices and Transparency

- Ethical marketing isn't just about following the law; it's about being honest and transparent with your audience.

 Misleading promotions, hidden affiliate links, or exaggerated claims can erode trust and lead to long-term damage to your brand.

- Solution:

 Be upfront about your affiliate relationships.

 Clearly disclose affiliate links and ensure that your content provides honest, unbiased reviews and recommendations.

 Always prioritize the needs and interests of your audience over quick profits.

Conclusion

As we look ahead to 2024 and 2025, affiliate marketing remains one of the most accessible and potentially lucrative ways to make money online.

The landscape is continuously evolving, with new technologies, trends, and challenges shaping the industry.

By staying informed, adaptable, and committed to providing value to your audience, you can build a successful affiliate marketing business that thrives in the years to come.

To summarize the key strategies for success:

- Choose a Niche Wisely:

 Select a niche that balances passion with profitability, and ensure there's a demand for the products you plan to promote.

- Build a Strong Platform:

 Invest in creating a well-designed, user-friendly website or blog, and consistently produce high-quality content that resonates with your audience.

- Drive Traffic and Optimize Conversions:

 Use a mix of SEO, social media, paid advertising, and email marketing to drive traffic. Optimize your content and affiliate links to maximize conversions.

- Scale and Diversify:

 As your business grows, diversify your content, affiliate programs, and income streams. Consider outsourcing and automation to manage your workload efficiently.

- Stay Ethical and Compliant:

　Adhere to legal requirements and ethical marketing practices.

　Build trust with your audience through transparency and honesty.

　The future of affiliate marketing is bright, with endless opportunities for those willing to put in the effort and stay ahead of the curve.

By focusing on the needs of your audience and continuously refining your strategies, you can achieve long-term success and enjoy the financial rewards that affiliate marketing has to offer.

This comprehensive guide provides you with the knowledge and tools to embark on or enhance your affiliate marketing journey in 2024 and 2025.

Remember, persistence, creativity, and a willingness to adapt are key ingredients in turning your affiliate marketing efforts into a thriving business.

Please use the next few pages for your notes and debates.

www.ingramcontent.com/pod-product-compliance
Lightning Source LLC
Chambersburg PA
CBHW071054240526
4547ICB00015B/1868